The Ku Klux Klan

By
Annie Cooper Burton

President, Wade Hampton Chapter, No. 763,
United Daughters of the Confederacy,
Los Angeles, California

Copyright, 1916

To Father

ISBN-13:
978-1979884563

ISBN-10:
1979884560

The Ku Klux Klan

The great Ku Klux Klan sprang up like a mushroom, a Southern organization formed in a time when no other power in the world could have saved the suffering South from the utter disorder which prevailed during the awful period following the War between the States.

The stigma attached to the name Ku Klux Klan by the uninformed masses has, at this late day, been practically removed, thanks to that Southern author, Thomas J. Dixon, who through "The Clansman" swayed public opinion the right way; and thanks again to that master director, David W. Griffith, another Southerner, who filmed this wonderful story and set the people to exclaiming, "Why, the Ku Klux Klan was a grand and noble order! It ranks with the best."

Every clubhouse of the United Daughters of the Confederacy should have a memorial tablet dedicated to the Ku Klux Klan; that would be a monument not to one man, but to five hundred and fifty thousand men, to whom all Southerners owe a debt of gratitude; for how our beloved Southland could have survived that reign of terror is a big question.

The very name Ku Klux shows that the order was formed among men of letters. It is a Greek word meaning circle. Klan suggested itself; the name complete in turn suggested mystery. Originally the order was purely a social organization, formed in Pulaski, Tennessee, May, 1866, and gave diversion to the restless young men after the reaction of war. They found vast amusement in belonging to a club which excited and baffled curiosity; great sport, too, was found in initiating new members. But it was when the Klan realized that it had a great, vital work to perform that it rose majestically to the gigantic task.

When the order at the end of a year had grown throughout the South to such a size that a master hand was needed to guide it, Nathan Bedford Forrest, famous cavalry general of the Southern Army, he of the charmed life, a man who was in "more than one hundred battles and had twenty-seven horses shot under him," a leader famous for his military strategy, was elected Grand Wizard of the Invisible Empire. Forrest always stressed the order that no fighting would be allowed. If they needed to fight they would throw off their disguise and fight like soldiers. Their purpose was to scare into submission the unruly free negroes and the trouble-making carpetbaggers; and this purpose they accomplished, without one drop of blood being shed, except in the most extreme cases. Whenever an undesirable citizen was not wanted, he generally found a note tacked to his door saying that if he did not move on within twenty-four hours he would be visited by the Ku Klux Klan. Signed "K. K. K." The man generally "moved on" long before the stipulated time.

The negroes, being naturally superstitious and imaginative, helped the order to gain power. In Nashville, Tennessee, among the five dens, there was one formed of medical students from the University. One of the favorite pranks of these young doctors was to ask a negro to hold their horse, and then place in his hand as he reached out to take the lines a finger or a hand taken from a corpse. The negro generally went a mile before he stopped running. Another effective trick practiced by the Klan was, when they had a negro on trial, to sprinkle beforehand a little powder on the floor—"hell fire," they called it—and when the negro would be looking down at the floor one of the Klansmen would surreptitiously run his foot over the powder line, and a fiery-looking trail would show. The negro would be paralyzed with fright, and was always careful in the future never to have cause to be brought before the Order again.

The Klan practiced numerous clever devices. Fancy the impression made on a negro when a robed Klansman asked him for a drink of water, to see a whole pail go down without any effort (a rubber bag concealed in the uniform aided in this deception), and then to hear a sepulchral voice say, "This is the first drink I have had since I was killed at Chickamauga!"

One never knew when nor where to expect a body of Ku Klux; they would spring up out of the ground, to all appearances; their ghostly figures multiplying like magic; they had a manner of forming their companies which made a band of one hundred men appear like a thousand. Their horses' feet were always muffled, making their approach completely noiseless. But it was only the guilty who feared them; and fear was what the Klan worked to effect. To kill was not their aim, and only where absolutely necessary was it ever resorted to. A rare instance was that of the hanging of a Northern spy by the Pulaski Klan. This man came to Pulaski and took up carpentry; he made the people like him, and worked himself into the Klan; got their pass-words, everything in fact that they knew; then made ready to get away to the North and expose the secrets of the Order. They found it out before he got away, and when he boarded the train in Pulaski, a number of the Klan boarded the car as it turned out of the city, took the man off the train and hung him at the bridge, thus saving their Order a gigantic tragedy. It was never known who did it, the government could find out nothing. The matter was never discussed by any of the Klan, even long years afterward.

In preparing this sketch of the Ku Klux Klan, I have been most fortunate in having Capt. H. W. Head, 9th Tennessee Regiment, now a popular physician of Santa Ana, California, a former Grand Cyclops of one of the Nashville dens, to draw upon for material, and through his generosity in lending me his treasured Prescript, which has never been out of his possession since 1867, I am enabled to give a verbatim copy of their secret oath and ritual. When Mrs. S. E. F. Rose, Historian of the Mississippi Division, wrote her interesting booklet on the Ku Klux Klan, she was anxious to secure a copy of this oath. She wrote to a lady in Tennessee who had one in her possession and asked if she would, for the sake of history, give her a copy. The lady replied that she regretted not being able to comply with her request, as she was not able to write it herself, and prized it too highly to allow it out of her possession for even an hour to have a typewritten copy made. She said that her Ku Klux papers, together with her husband's parole of honor obtained at Appomatox, Virginia, were to her treasures whose price was far above rubies. So you see what a treasure we have secured through Capt. Head's gallantry and generosity. I am sure the Daughters appreciate the interest he has taken in helping compile this data. It was my aim to get information first-hand.

My father, Capt. James C. Cooper, was Grand Cyclops of a den in Mt. Pleasant, Tennessee, but I never saw his uniform, as it was burned when the Klan disbanded. Capt. Head buried his uniform, and thus saved it. He obliged me by posing for a photograph in this interesting outfit. It was strange how the old feeling came back to him. He felt, he said, as if he were breaking his secret oath in thus displaying his uniform. Certainly he did look guilty and a little self-conscious as he emerged from the funny-looking garment. The buttons you see so generously distributed are made of tin; the cloth is of black calico with white trimmings; the only color used is a touch of red around the mouth and over the eyes. A woman, who was sworn to secrecy, was generally appointed by the dens to make their uniforms, so that they would all be alike.

As in Masonry, no one was asked outright to join the Klan. If a man happened to be talking to a Klansman and showed a kindly interest in the Order and a desire to join it, the Klansman would talk around the subject, and if the man was of good character, would suggest that they might find out something about it, the Klansman hinting that he thought he knew some one who belonged to it, and who might get them into the Order. Capt. Head had a funny experience with his own father. They were talking one day about the new Order when the father asked: "Do you know who these people are who call themselves the Ku Klux Klan?" The son replied that he might be able to take him to a place where they could find out. At the next meeting of his den, Capt. Head asked his father to go with him, an invitation which was accepted. The old gentleman was blindfolded and plied with the regulation questions, all of which he answered satisfactorily. When the blindfold was removed he was greatly surprised and pleased to see two of his own sons members of the den, Capt. Head himself taking his father into the Order.

The Ku Klux Klan lasted for three years; they disbanded as quietly and as quickly as they formed. When martial law was declared, and the work was done, Forrest sent out this order, through word of mouth, from den to den, throughout the vast Empire:

"The Invisible Empire has accomplished the purpose for which it was organized. Civil law now affords ample protection to life, liberty and property; robbery and lawlessness are no longer unrebuked; the better elements of society are no longer in dread for the safety of their property, their persons, and their families. The Grand Wizard, being invested with power to determine questions of paramount importance, in the exercise of the power so conferred, now declares the Invisible Empire and all the subdivisions thereof dissolved and disbanded forever."

Uniforms, oaths, and rituals were ordered burned, because it meant death to a Klansman to have them found in his possession, so strong had grown the feeling against the Order, due to unscrupulous outsiders who committed horrible deeds in the guise of the Klan. But the grand old Order had accomplished what it set out to do. Its work was nobly done; and our rescued South still sings her gratitude to her heaven-sent protectors, the mysterious K. K. K.

APPELLATION

This Organization shall be styled and denominated, The Order of the (then follows three stars; no other name given).

CREED

We, the Order of the * * *, reverentially acknowledge the majesty and supremacy of the Divine Being, and recognize the goodness and providence of the same. And we recognize our relation to the United States Government, the supremacy of the Constitution, the Constitutional Laws thereof, and the Union of States thereunder.

CHARACTER AND OBJECTS OF THE ORDER

This is an institution of Chivalry, Humanity, Mercy, and Patriotism; embodying in its genius and its principles all that is chivalric in conduct, noble in sentiment, generous in manhood, and patriotic in purpose; its peculiar object being,

First: To protect the weak, the innocent, and the defenseless, from the indignities, wrongs, and outrages, of the lawless, the violent, and the brutal; to relieve the injured and oppressed; to succor the suffering and unfortunate, and especially the widows and orphans of Confederate soldiers.

Second: To protect and defend the Constitution of the United States, and all laws passed in conformity thereto, and to protect the States and the people thereof from all invasion from any source, whatever.

Nec seire fas est omnia.

Third: To aid and assist in the execution of all constitutional laws, and to protect the people from unlawful seizure, and from trial except by their peers in conformity to the laws of the land.

ARTICLE I.

Titles

Section 1. The officers of the Order shall consist of a Grand Wizard of the Empire, and his ten Genii; a Grand Dragon of the Realm, and his eight Hydras; a Grand Titan of the Dominion, and his six Furies; a Grand Giant of the Province, and his four Goblins; a Grand Cyclops of the Den, and his two Nighthawks; a Grand Magi, a Grand Monk, a Grand Scribe, a Grand Exchequer, a Grand Turk, and a Grand Sentinel.

Section 2. The body politic of the Order shall be known and designated as "Ghouls."

ARTICLE II.

Territory and Its Divisions

Section 1. The territory embraced within the jurisdiction of this Order shall be coterminous with the States of Maryland, Virginia, North Carolina, South Carolina, Georgia, Florida, Alabama, Mississippi, Louisiana, Texas, Arkansas, Missouri, Kentucky, and Tennessee; all combined constituting the Empire.

Section 2. The Empire shall be divided into four departments, the first to be styled the Realm, and coterminous with the boundaries of the several States; the second to be styled the Dominion, and

Amiei humani generis.

---

to be coterminous with such counties as the Grand Dragons of the several Realms may assign to the charge of the Grand Titan. The third to be styled the Province, and to be coterminous with the several counties; **provided**, the Grand Titan may, when he deems it necessary, assign two Grand Giants to one Province, prescribing, at the same time, the jurisdiction of each. The fourth department to be styled the Den, and shall embrace such part of a Province as the Grand Giant shall assign to the charge of a Grand Cyclops.

ARTICLE III.

Powers and Duties of Officers

Grand Wizard

Section 1. The Grand Wizard, who is the supreme officer of the Empire, shall have power, and he shall be required, to appoint Grand Dragons for the different Realms of the Empire; and he shall have power to appoint his Genii, also a Grand Scribe, and a Grand Exchequer for his Department, and he shall have the sole power to issue copies of this Prescript, through his Subalterns, for the organization and dissemination of the Order; and when a question of paramount importance to the interests or prosperity of the Order arises, not provided for in this Prescript, he shall have the power to determine such question, and his decision shall be final until the same shall be provided for by amendment as hereinafter provided. It shall be his duty to communicate with, and receive reports from the Grand Dragons of Realms as to the condition, strength, and progress of the Order within their respective Realms. And

Quemcunque miserum videris, hominem scias.

---

it shall further be his duty to keep, by his Grand Scribe, a list of the names (without any caption or explanation whatever) of the Grand Dragons of the different Realms of the Empire, and shall number such Realms with the Arabic numerals 1, 2, 3, etc., **ad finem**; and he shall direct and instruct his Grand Exchequer as to the appropriation and disbursement he shall make of the revenue of the Order that comes to his hands.

Grand Dragon

Sec. 2. The Grand Dragon, who is the chief officer of the Realm, shall have power, and he shall be required, to appoint and instruct a Grand Titan for each Dominion of his Realm, (such Dominion not to exceed three in number for any Congressional District) said appointments being subject to the approval of the Grand Wizard of the Empire. He shall have power to appoint his Hydras; also a Grand Scribe and a Grand Exchequer for his Department.

It shall be his duty to report to the Grand Wizard, when required by that officer, the condition, strength, efficiency, and progress of the Order within his Realm, and to transmit, through the Grand Titan, or other authorized sources, to the Order, all information, intelligence, or instruction conveyed to him by the Grand Wizard for that purpose, and all such other information or instruction as he may think will promote the interest and utility of the Order. He shall keep by his Grand Scribe, a list of the names (without caption) of the Grand Titans of the different Dominions of his Realm, and shall report the same to the Grand Wizard when required, and

Magna est veritas, et prevalebit.

shall number the Dominions of his Realm with the Arabic numerals, 1, 2, 3, etc., **ad finem**. And he shall direct and instruct his Grand Exchequer as to the appropriation and disbursement he shall make of the revenue of the Order that comes to his hands.

Grand Titan

Sec 3. The Grand Titan, who is the chief officer of the Dominion, shall have power, and he shall be required, to appoint and instruct a Grand Giant for each Province of his Dominion, such appointments, however, being subject to the approval of the Grand Dragon of the Realm. He shall have the power to appoint his Furies; also, a Grand Scribe and a Grand Exchequer for his Department. It shall be his duty to report to the Grand Dragon when required by that officer, the condition, strength, efficiency, and progress of the Order within his Dominion, and to transmit through the Grand Giant, or other authorized channels, to the Order, all information, intelligence, instruction or directions conveyed to him by the Grand Dragon for that purpose, and all such other information or instruction as he may think will enhance the interest or efficiency of the Order.

He shall keep, by his Grand Scribe, a list of the names (without caption or explanation) of the Grand Giants of the different Provinces of his Dominion, and shall report the same to the Grand Dragon when required; and shall number the Provinces of his Dominion with the Arabic numerals, 1, 2, 3, etc., **ad finem**. And he shall direct and instruct his Grand Exchequer as to the appropriation and disbursement he shall make of the revenue of the Order that comes to his hands.

Ne tentes aut perfice.

Grand Giant

Sec. 4. The Grand Giant, who is the chief officer of the Province, shall have power, and he is required, to appoint and instruct a Grand Cyclops for each Den of his Province, such appointments, however, being subject to the approval of the Grand Titan of the Dominion. And he shall have the further power to appoint his Goblins; also, a Grand Scribe and a Grand Exchequer for his Department.

It shall be his duty to supervise and administer general and special instructions in the organization and establishment of the Order within his Province, and to report to the Grand Titan, when required by that officer, the condition, strength, efficiency, and progress of the Order within his Province, and to transmit through the Grand Cyclops, or other legitimate sources, to the Order, all information, intelligence, instruction, or directions conveyed to him by the Grand Titan or other higher authority for that purpose, and all such other information or instruction as he may think would advance the purposes or prosperity of the Order. He shall keep, by his Grand Scribe, a list of the

names (without caption or explanation) of the Grand
Cyclops of the various Dens of his Province, and shall
report the same to the Grand Titan when required; and shall
number the Dens of his Province with the Arabic numerals
1, 2, 3, etc., **ad finem**. He shall determine and limit the
number of Dens to be organized and established in his
Province; and he shall direct and instruct his Grand
Exchequer as to the appropriation and disbursement he
shall make of the revenue of the Order that comes to his
hands.

Quid faciendum?

Grand Cyclops

Sec. 5. The Grand Cyclops, who is the chief officer of the
Den, shall have power to appoint his Nighthawks, his
Grand Scribe, his Grand Turk, his Grand Exchequer, and
his Grand Sentinel. And for small offenses he may punish
any member by fine, and may reprimand him for the same.
And he is further empowered to admonish and reprimand
his Den, or any of the members thereof, for any
imprudence, irregularity, or transgression, whenever he
may think that the interests, welfare, reputation, or safety of
the Order demands it. It shall be his duty to take charge of
his Den under the instruction and with the assistance (when
practicable) of the Grand Giant, and in accordance with and
in conformity to the provisions of this Prescript,—a copy of
which shall in all cases be obtained before the formation of
a Den begins. It shall further be his duty to appoint all
regular meetings of his Den, and to preside at the same; to
appoint irregular meetings when he deems it expedient; to
preserve order and enforce discipline in his Den; to impose
fines for irregularities or disobedience of orders; and to

receive and initiate candidates for admission into the Order, after the same shall have been pronounced competent and worthy to become members, by the Investigating Committee hereinafter provided for. And it shall further be his duty to make a quarterly report to the Grand Giant of the condition, strength, efficiency, and progress of his Den, and shall communicate to the Officers and Ghouls of his Den, all information, intelligence, instruction, or direction, conveyed to him by the Grand Giant or other higher authority for that

Fiat justicia coelum.

---

purpose; and shall from time to time administer all other counsel, instruction or direction, as in his sound discretion, will conduce to the interests, and more effectually accomplish, the real objects and designs of the Order.

Grand Magi

Sec. 6. It shall be the duty of the Grand Magi, who is the second officer in authority of the Den, to assist the Grand Cyclops, and to obey all the orders of that officer; to preside at all meetings in the Den, in the absence of the Grand Cyclops; and to discharge during his absence all the duties and exercise all the powers and authority of that officer.

Grand Monk

Sec. 7. It shall be the duty of the Grand Monk, who is the third officer in authority of the Den, to assist and obey all the orders of the Grand Cyclops and the Grand Magi; and in the absence of both of these officers he shall preside at and conduct the meetings in the Den, and shall discharge all the duties, and exercise all the powers and authority of the Grand Cyclops.

Grand Exchequer

Sec. 8. It shall be the duty of the Grand Exchequers of the different Departments to keep a correct account of all the revenue of the Order that comes to their hands, and of all paid out by them; and shall make no appropriation or disbursement of the same except under the orders and direction of

Dormitus aliquando jus, moritus nunquam.

---

the chief officer of their respective Departments. And it shall further be the duty of the Exchequers of Dens to collect the initiation fees, and all fines imposed by the Grand Cyclops, or the officer discharging his functions.

Grand Turk

Sec. 9. It shall be the duty of the Grand Turk, who is the executive officer of the Grand Cyclops, to notify the Officers and Ghouls of the Den, of all informal or irregular meetings appointed by the Grand Cyclops, and to obey and execute all the orders of that officer in the control and government of his Den. It shall further be his duty to receive and question at the outposts, all candidates for admission into the Order, and shall **there** administer the preliminary obligation required, and then conduct such candidate or candidates to the Grand Cyclops, and to assist him in the initiation of the same.

Grand Scribe

Sec. 10. It shall be the duty of the Grand Scribes of the different Departments to conduct the correspondence and write the orders of the Chiefs of their Departments, when required. And it shall further be the duty of the Grand Scribes of Dens, to keep a list of the names (without any caption or explanation whatever) of the Officers and Ghouls of the Den, to call the roll at all meetings, and to make the quarterly reports under the direction and instruction of the Grand Cyclops.

Quieta no movere.

Grand Sentinel

Sec. 11. It shall be the duty of the Grand Sentinel to take charge of post and instruct the Grand Guard, under the direction and orders of the Grand Cyclops, and to relieve and dismiss the same when directed by that officer.

The Staff

Sec. 12. The Genii shall constitute the staff of the Grand Wizard; the Hydras, that of the Grand Dragon; the Furies, that of the Grand Titan; the Goblins, that of the Grand Giant; and the Nighthawks, that of the Grand Cyclops.

Removal

Sec. 13. For any just, reasonable, and substantial cause, any appointee may be removed by the authority that appointed him, and his place supplied by another appointment.

ARTICLE IV.

Election of Officers

Section 1. The Grand Wizard shall be elected biennially by the Grand Dragons of Realms. The first election for this office to take place on the first Monday in May, 1870 (a Grand Wizard having been created, by the original Prescript, to serve three years from the first Monday in May 1867); all subsequent elections to take place every two years thereafter. And the incumbent Grand Wizard shall notify the Grand Dragons of the different Realms, at least six months before said election, at what time

Quid verum atque decens.

---

and place the same shall be held; a majority vote of all the Grand Dragons present being necessary and sufficient to elect a Grand Wizard. Such election shall be by ballot, and shall be held by three Commissioners appointed by the Grand Wizard for that purpose; and in the event of a tie, the Grand Wizard shall have the casting vote.

Sec. 2. The Grand Magi and the Grand Monk of Dens shall be elected annually by the Ghouls of Dens; and the first election for these officers may take place as soon as ten Ghouls have been initiated for the formation of a Den. All subsequent elections to take place every year thereafter.

Sec. 3. In the event of a vacancy in the office of Grand Wizard, by death, resignation, removal, or otherwise, the senior Grand Dragon of the Empire shall immediately assume and enter upon the discharge of the duties of the Grand Wizard, and shall exercise the powers and perform the duties of said office until the same shall be filled by election; and the said senior Grand Dragon, as soon as practicable after the happening of such vacancy, shall call a convention of the Grand Dragons of the Realms, to be held at such time and place as in his discretion he may deem most convenient and proper. **Provided**, however, that the time for assembling such convention for the election of a Grand Wizard shall in no case exceed six months from the time such vacancy occurred; and in the event of a vacancy in any other office, the same shall immediately be filled in the manner hereinbefore mentioned.

Sec. 4. The Officers heretofore elected or appointed may retain their offices during the time for

Art est colare artem.

---

which they have been so elected or appointed, at the expiration of which time said offices shall be filled as hereinbefore provided.

ARTICLE V.

Judiciary

Section 1. The Tribunal of Justice of this Order shall consist of a Court at the Headquarters of the Empire, the Realm, the Dominion, the Province, and the Den, to be appointed by the Chiefs of these several Departments.

Sec. 2. The Court at the Headquarters of the Empire shall consist of three Judges for the trial of Grand Dragons, and the Officers and attaches belonging to the Headquarters of the Empire.

Sec. 3. The Court at the Headquarters of the Realm shall consist of three Judges for the trial of Grand Titans, and the Officers and attaches belonging to the Headquarters of the Realm.

Sec. 4. The Court at the Headquarters of the Dominion shall consist of three Judges for the trial of Grand Giants, and the Officers and attaches belonging to the Headquarters of the Dominion.

Sec. 5. The Court at the Headquarters of the Province shall consist of five Judges for the trial of Grand Cyclops, the Grand Magis, the Grand Monks, and the Grand Exchequers of Dens, and the Officers and attaches belonging to the Headquarters of the Province.

Sec. 6. The Court at the Headquarters of the Den shall consist of seven Judges appointed from

Nusquam tuta fides.

---

the Den for the trial of Ghouls and the Officers belonging to the Headquarters of the Den.

Sec. 7. The Tribunal for the trial of the Grand Wizard shall be composed of at least seven Grand Dragons, to be convened by the senior Grand Dragon upon charges being preferred against the Grand Wizard; which Tribunal shall be organized and presided over by the senior Grand Dragon **present**; and if they find the accused guilty, they shall prescribe the penalty, and the senior Grand Dragons of the Empire shall cause the same to be executed.

Sec. 8. The aforesaid Courts shall summon the accused and witnesses for and against him, and if found guilty, they shall prescribe the penalty, and the Officers convening the Court shall cause the same to be executed. **Provided**, the accused shall always have the right of appeal to the next Court above, whose decision shall be final.

Sec. 9. The Judges constituting the aforesaid Courts shall be selected with reference to their intelligence, integrity, and fair-mindedness and shall render their verdict without prejudice, favor, partiality, or affection, and shall be so sworn, upon the organization of the Court; and shall further be sworn to administer even-handed justice.

Sec. 10. The several Courts herein provided for shall be governed in their deliberations, proceedings, and judgments by the rules and regulations governing the proceedings of regular Court-martial.

Fide non armis.

ARTICLE VI.

Revenue

Section 1. The revenue of this Order shall be derived as follows: For every copy of this Prescript issued to Dens $10 will be required; $2 of which shall go into the hands of the Grand Exchequer of the Grand Giant; $2 into the hands of Grand Exchequer of the Grand Titan; $2 into the hands of the Grand Exchequer of the Grand Dragon, and the remaining $4 into the hands of the Grand Exchequer of the Grand Wizard.

Sec. 2. A further source of revenue to the Empire shall be ten per cent. of all the revenue of the Realms, and a tax upon Realms when the Grand Wizard shall deem it necessary and indispensable to levy the same.

Sec. 3. A further source of revenue to Realms shall be ten per cent. of all the revenue of Dominions, and a tax upon Dominions when the Grand Dragon shall deem it necessary and indispensable to levy the same.

Sec. 4. A further source of revenue to Dominions shall be ten per cent. of all the revenue of Provinces, and a tax upon Provinces when the Grand Giant shall deem such tax necessary and indispensable.

Sec. 5. A further source of revenue to Provinces shall be ten per cent. of all the revenue of Dens, and a tax upon Dens when the Grand Giant shall deem such tax necessary and indispensable.

Dat Deus his quoque finem.

Sec. 6. The source of revenue to Dens shall be the initiation fees, fines, and a **per capita** tax, whenever the Grand Cyclops shall deem such tax necessary and indispensable to the interests and objects of the Order.

Sec. 7. All the revenue obtained in the manner aforesaid, shall be for the **exclusive** benefit of the Order, and shall be appropriated to the dissemination of the same and to the creation of a fund to meet any disbursement that it may become necessary to make to accomplish the objects of the Order and to secure the protection of the same.

ARTICLE VII.

Eligibility for Membership

Section 1. No one shall be pressed for admission into the Order until he shall have first been recommended by some friend or intimate who is a member, to the Investigating Committee (which shall be composed of the Grand Cyclops, the Grand Magi, and the Grand Monk), and who shall have investigated his antecedents and his past and present standing and connections, and after such investigation, shall have pronounced him competent and worthy to become a member. **Provided**, no one shall be presented for admission into, or become a member of this Order, who shall not have attained the age of eighteen years.

Sec. 2. No one shall become a member of this Order unless he shall **voluntarily** take the following oaths or obligations, and shall **satisfactorily** answer the following interrogatories, while kneeling, with

Cessante causa, cessat effectus.

---

his right hand raised to heaven, and his left hand resting on the Bible.

Preliminary Obligation

"I —— solemnly swear or affirm that I will never reveal anything that I may this day (or night) learn concerning the Order of the * * * and that I will true answer make to such interrogatories as may be put to me touching my competency for admission into the same. So help me God."

Interrogatories to Be Asked

1st. Have you ever been rejected, upon application for membership in the * * *, or have you ever been expelled from the same?

2nd. Are you now, or have you ever been, a member of the Radical Republican party, or either of the organizations known as the "Loyal League" and the "Grand Army of the Republic?"

3rd. Are you opposed to the principles and policy of the Radical party, and to the Loyal League, and the Grand Army of the Republic, so far as you are informed of the character and purposes of these organizations?

4th. Did you belong to the Federal army during the late war, and fight against the South during the existence of the same?

5th. Are you opposed to negro equality, both social and political?

6th. Are you in favor of a white man's Government in this country?

Cave quid, dicis, quando, et cui.

7th. Are you in favor of Constitutional liberty and a Government of equitable laws instead of a Government of violence and oppression?

8th. Are you in favor of maintaining the Constitutional rights of the South?

9th. Are you in favor of the re-enfranchisement and emancipation of the white men of the South, and the restitution of the Southern people to all their rights, alike proprietary, civil, and political?

10th. Do you believe in the inalienable right of self-preservation of the people against the exercise of arbitrary and unlicensed power?

If the foregoing interrogatories are satisfactorily answered, and the candidate desires to go further (after something of the character and nature of the Order has thus been indicated to him) and to be admitted to the benefits, mysteries, secrets, and purposes of the Order, he shall then be required to take the following final oath or obligation. But if said interrogatories are not satisfactorily answered, or the candidate declines to proceed further, he shall be discharged, after being solemnly admonished by the initiating officer of the deep secrecy to which the oath already taken has bound him, and that the extreme penalty of the law will follow a violation of thc same.

Final Obligation

"I —— of my own free will and accord, and in the presence of Almighty God, do solemnly swear or affirm, that I will never reveal to any one, not even a member of the Order of the * * *, by any intimation, sign, symbol, word or act, or in any

Nemo tenetur seipsum accura.

other manner whatever, any of the secrets, signs, grips, pass-words, or mysteries of the Order of the * * *, or that I am a member of the same, or that I know any one who is a member; and that I will abide by the Prescript and Edicts of the Order of the * * *. So help me God."

The initiating officer will then proceed to explain to the new member the character and objects of the Order, and introduce him to the mysteries and secrets of the same; and shall read to him this Prescript and the Edicts thereof, or present the same to him for personal perusal.

ARTICLE VIII.

Amendments

This Prescript or any part of the Edicts thereof shall never be changed, except by a two-thirds vote of the Grand Dragons of the Realms, in convention assembled, and at which convention the Grand Wizard shall preside and be entitled to a vote. And upon the application of a majority of the Grand Dragons for that purpose, the Grand Wizard shall call and appoint the time and place for said convention; which, when assembled, shall proceed to make such modifications and amendments as it may think will promote the interest, enlarge the utility, and more thoroughly effectuate the purposes of the Order.

ARTICLE IX.

Interdiction

The origin, mysteries, and Ritual of this Order shall never be written, but the same shall be communicated orally.

Deo adjuvante, non timendum.

ARTICLE X.

Edicts

1. No one shall become a member of a distant Den, where there is a Den established and in operation in his own immediate vicinity; nor shall any one become a member of any Den, or of this Order in any way, after he shall have been once rejected, upon application for membership.

2. No Den, or officer, or member, or members thereof, shall operate beyond their prescribed limits, unless invited or ordered by the proper authority to do so.

3. No member shall be allowed to take any intoxicating spirits to any meeting of the Den; nor shall any member be allowed to attend a meeting while intoxicated; and for every appearance at a meeting in such condition he shall be fined the sum of not less than one nor more than five dollars, to go into the revenue of the Order.

4. Any member may be expelled from the Order by a majority vote of the Officers and Ghouls of the Den to which he belongs; and if after such expulsion, such member shall assume any of the duties, regalia, or insignia of the Order, or in any way claim to be a member of the same, he shall be severely punished. His obligation of secrecy shall be as binding upon him after his expulsion as before, and for any revelation made by him thereafter, he shall be held accountable in the same manner as if he were then a member.

5. Upon the expulsion of any member from the Order, the Grand Cyclops, or the Officer acting in

---

his stead, shall immediately report the same to the Grand Giant of the Province, who shall cause the fact to be made known and read in each Den of his Province, and shall transmit the same, through the proper channels, to the Grand Dragon of the Realm, who shall cause it to be published to every Den in the Realm, and shall notify the Grand Dragons of contiguous Realms of the same.

6. Every Grand Cyclops shall read, or cause to be read, this Prescript and these Edicts to his Den, at least once in every month; and shall read them to each new member when he is initiated, or present the same to him for his personal perusal.

7. The initiation fee of this Order shall be one dollar, to be paid when the candidate is initiated and received into the Order.

8. Dens may make such additional Edicts for their control and government as they may deem requisite and necessary. **Provided**, no Edict shall be made to conflict with any of the provisions or Edicts of this Prescript.

9. The most profound and rigid secrecy concerning any and everything that relates to the Order, shall at all times be maintained.

10. Any member who shall reveal or betray the secrets of this Order, shall suffer the extreme penalty of the law.

Admonition

Hush! thou art not to utter what I am; bethink thee, it was our covenant!

Nemo nos impune lacissit.

REGISTER

I.

1.Dismal,   7. Painful,
2.Mystic,   8. Portentous,
3.Stormy,   9. Fading,
4.Peculiar,   10.Melancholy,
5.Blooming,11.Glorious,
6.Brilliant, 12.Gloomy.

II.

I. White, II. Green, III. Yellow, IV. Amber, V. Purple, VI. Crimson, VII. Emerald.

III.

1.Fearful,   7. Hideous,
2.Startling,   8. Frightful,
3.Wonderful,9. Awful,
4.Alarming,   10.Horrible,
5.Mournful,   11.Dreadful,
6.Appalling, 12.Last.

IV.

Cumberland.

L'ENVOI

To the lovers of law and order, peace and justice, we send greeting; and to the shades of the venerated dead we affectionately dedicate the Order, of the * * *.

Ad unum omnes.

RESURGAMUS